Worship HYMNS FOR ORGAN

The Golden Jubilee Collection

This collection commemorates the music and ministry of
Carolyn Hamlin

Worship HYMNS FOR ORGAN

FOREWORD

When our Music Advisory Council first began working on plans for a fitting celebration of Carolyn Hamlin's 50th anniversary as church organist, the challenge quickly became how to narrow the ideas down to those which would honor Carolyn and acknowledge the depth of her ministry at First Baptist Church, Easley, SC. As the discussion proceeded, we soon agreed on what would mean the most to her. After nearly four years of planning, you now hold in your hands the result of that decision. We believe this collection, *Worship Hymns for Organ - Golden Jubilee Collection* was the crowning achievement of that anniversary celebration weekend in 2008.

In July 2008, Carolyn Hamlin marked fifty years of faithful service to our congregation. Fifty years is a long time to maintain such a high level of commitment to the families of our church. Along the way, Carolyn maintained a high standard of musical excellence as she touched thousands of lives throughout our community. Through her leadership in Sunday worship services, funerals, weddings, revivals, concerts, seminars, children's choirs, youth choirs, and adult choirs, she connected the promises of Holy Scripture through traditional hymnody to real seasons of life .

In recent years, new doors of ministry have opened for Carolyn as she has answered God's call to share her music through choral and organ compositions. Organists around the country have been inspired not only by her music, but by her leadership in various organ/worship seminars all over the United States. More than any other person in the life of our church, Carolyn Hamlin's name is synonymous with First Baptist Church, Easley.

During that anniversary weekend, we said "thank you" in many ways: a reunion choir; an Honorary Doctorate from her alma mater; a banquet in her honor; a church-wide dinner; a concert featuring Carolyn's organ and choral compositions; a love offering; a Carolyn Hamlin Music Scholarship; a book of memories; three commissioned choral anthems, and South Carolina's second highest civilian award, the Order of the Silver Crescent.

Working with some of the finest contemporary composers of organ literature in the world and a publisher who understands not only the changing face of Christian worship, but the tried and tested expressions as well, we believe that we have commissioned one of the seminal anthologies of contemporary organ literature available today. Our hope is that this collection will adequately reflect our love for Carolyn and her love for the Christ she so faithfully serves from the organ console. May this album also inspire others with similar gifts and passions to answer the call to music ministry and keep the "king of instruments" an integral part of contemporary worship.

The words of St. Paul himself express our gratitude: Carolyn, we "thank our God every time we remember you. In all our prayers for you, we always pray with joy because of your partnership in the gospel from the first day until now, being confident of this, that he who began a good work in you will carry it on to completion until the day of Christ Jesus." We know that God is not finished with her ministry here at First Baptist Church and pray for many more years of shared ministry.

Rick Baumgarner
Minister of Music
First Baptist Church
Easley, SC

Worship HYMNS FOR ORGAN

Table of Contents

MORE LOVE TO THEE, O CHRIST (Arr. Carolyn Hamlin) 4

VARIATIONS ON "WYVE VALLEY" (Arr. Joyce Jones) 10

HYMN OF MAJESTY AND POWER (Arr. Mark Thallander) 18

TOCCATA ON "HYMN TO JOY" (Arr. Joel Martinson) 21

TOCCATA ON "MENDELSSOHN" (Arr. Craig Phillips) 28

VARIATIONS ON "ADESTE FIDELES" (Arr. Frederick Swann) 38

THE PROMISED LAND (Arr. Trey Clegg) 46

AND CAN IT BE (Arr. Anna Laura Page) 54

THE SOLID ROCK (Arr. Michael Burkhardt) 62

NOW THANK WE ALL OUR GOD (Arr. Diane Bish) 70

Fred Bock Music Company

www.FredBock.com
www.worshiphymnsfororgan.com

dedicated to the international concert organist, Carlo Curley

MORE LOVE TO THEE, O CHRIST

WILLIAM H. DOANE
Arranged by CAROLYN HAMLIN

General [1]
Sw. Salicional 8', Salicional Celeste 8'
Gt. Waldorn 8'
Ch. Erzahler 8', Erzahler Celeste 8', Sw. to Ch. 8'
Ped. Violone 16', Sw. to Ped.

General [2]
Sw. Flute Celeste
Gt. Flute Harmonic, Sw. to Gt. 8', Ch. to Gt. 8'
Ch. Viole, Viole Celeste, Sw. to Ch. 8'
Ped. Choral Bass 4' (Ped. [1] Violone 16')

General [3]
Sw. Salicional 8', Salicional Celeste 8', Flute 8'
Gt. Diapason 8', Harmonic Flute 8', Sw. to Gt. 8', Ch. to Gt. 8'
Ch. Flute 8', Flute Celeste 8', Viole 8', Viole Celeste 8'
Ped. Bourdon 16', Ch. to Ped.

General [4]
Sw. Salicional 8', Salicional Celeste 8', Vox Humana 8', Trem.
Gt. Gamba 8', Trem., Sw. to Gt. 8', Ch. to Gt. 8'
Ch. Viole 8', Viole Celeste 8', Trem.
Ped. Violone 16', Lieblich Bourdon 16', Sw. to Ped., Ch. to Ped.

General [5]
Sw. Bourdon 8', Viola 8', Principal 4'
Gt. Diapason 8', Harmonic Flute 8', Octave 4', Sw. to Gt. 16', 8'
Ch. Festival Trumpet
Ped. Diapason 16', Bourdon 16', Violone 16', Flute 8', Gt. to Ped., Sw. to Ped.

General [6]
Sw. Viola 8', Principal 4', Mix. IV, Bassoon 16', Trumpet 8', Clarion 4'
Gt. Violone 16', Diapason 8', 4', 2', Twelfth 2-2/3, Sw. to Gt. 8', Ch. to Gt. 8'
Ch. Gedeckt 8', Koppelflute 4', Principal 4', Mix. III
Ped. Bourdon 32', Diapason 16', Bourdon 16', Octave 8', Bombarde 16', Gt. to Ped., Sw. to Ped.

General [7]
Sw. Salicional 8', Salicional Celeste 8'
Gt. Waldhorn 8'
Ch. Viole, Viole Celeste, Sw. to Ch. 8'
Ped. Lieblich Gedeckt 16'

General [8]
Sw. Hautbois
Ch. Erzahler 8', Erzahler Celeste 8' (Ch. [1] Flute Celeste)
Ped. Lieblich Gedeckt 16'
(Ped. [2] Lieblich Gedeckt 16', Soft 32')

With much expression (♩ = 68)

9
13
Ch.
slight rit.
17
Sw.
a tempo
Gt.
21
Sw.
slight rit.

24
Gen. [2]
Sw.
a tempo
slight rit.
28
a tempo
slight rit.
32
Gt.
a tempo
36
Ch.

40
Gt.
Ped. [1]
43
Gen. [3]
Gt.
slight rit.
47
Gen. [4]
Gt.
a little slower
51

55
Gen. [5]
Gt.
Ch.
59
rit.
62
Gen. [6]
Gt.
Much broader
65
Much slower
Full organ w/Reeds

68
71
Gen. [7]
Ch.
Gt.
74
rit.
Ch.
77
Gen. [8]
Ch.
Sw.
Sw.
Ch. [1]
Ch.
pp
Ped. [2]

to Carolyn, in appreciation for your dedicated ministry through music and your friendship

VARIATIONS ON "WYE VALLEY"

Sw. Strings 8'
Gt. Flute 8'
Ch. Flute 8', 2-2/3', 1-3/5'
Ped. Soft 16', 8'

JAMES MOUNTAIN
Arranged by JOYCE JONES

13
♩ = 96
Sw. Oboe 8'
Gt.
17
21
25

29
Gt.
Ch.
Gt.
33
37
41

45
48
52
Sw. Strings 8'
Ped. Soft 16', 8'
𝅗𝅥 = 72
56

60
♩ = 104
Gt. Flute 8'
Sw.
Solo Oboe, Clarinet or Principal 4' only
64
67
70

73
76
Sw. Flutes & Strings 8', 4'
Ped. Soft 16', 8'
= 76
79
Sw.
82
+ Sw. Foundations 8', 4', 2'
Increase to Gt. 8', 4', 2'
Full Sw. to Gt.
Pedal Foundations 16', 8', 4'
Gt. & Sw. to Pedal

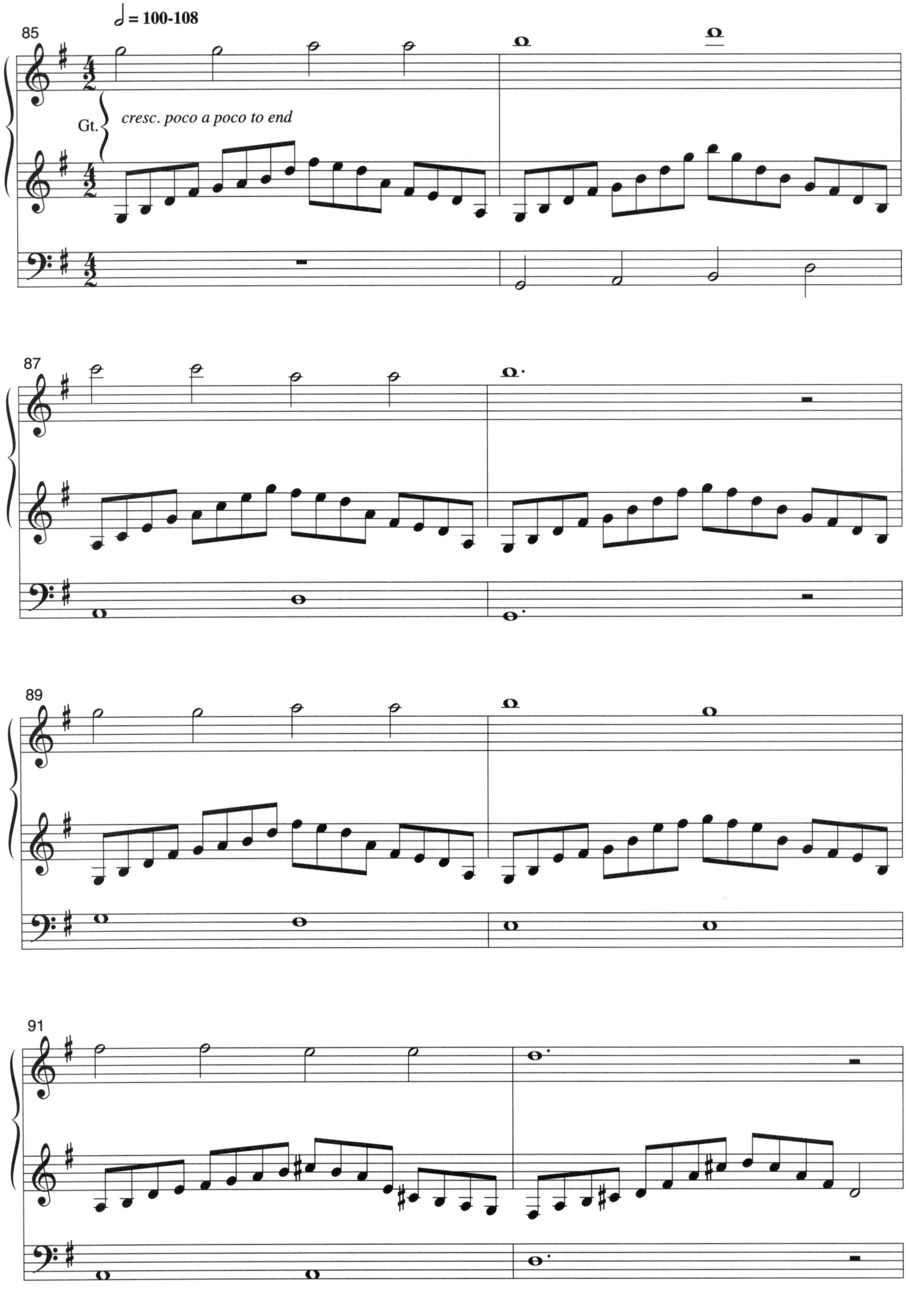
= 100-108
85
Gt.
cresc. poco a poco to end
87
89
91

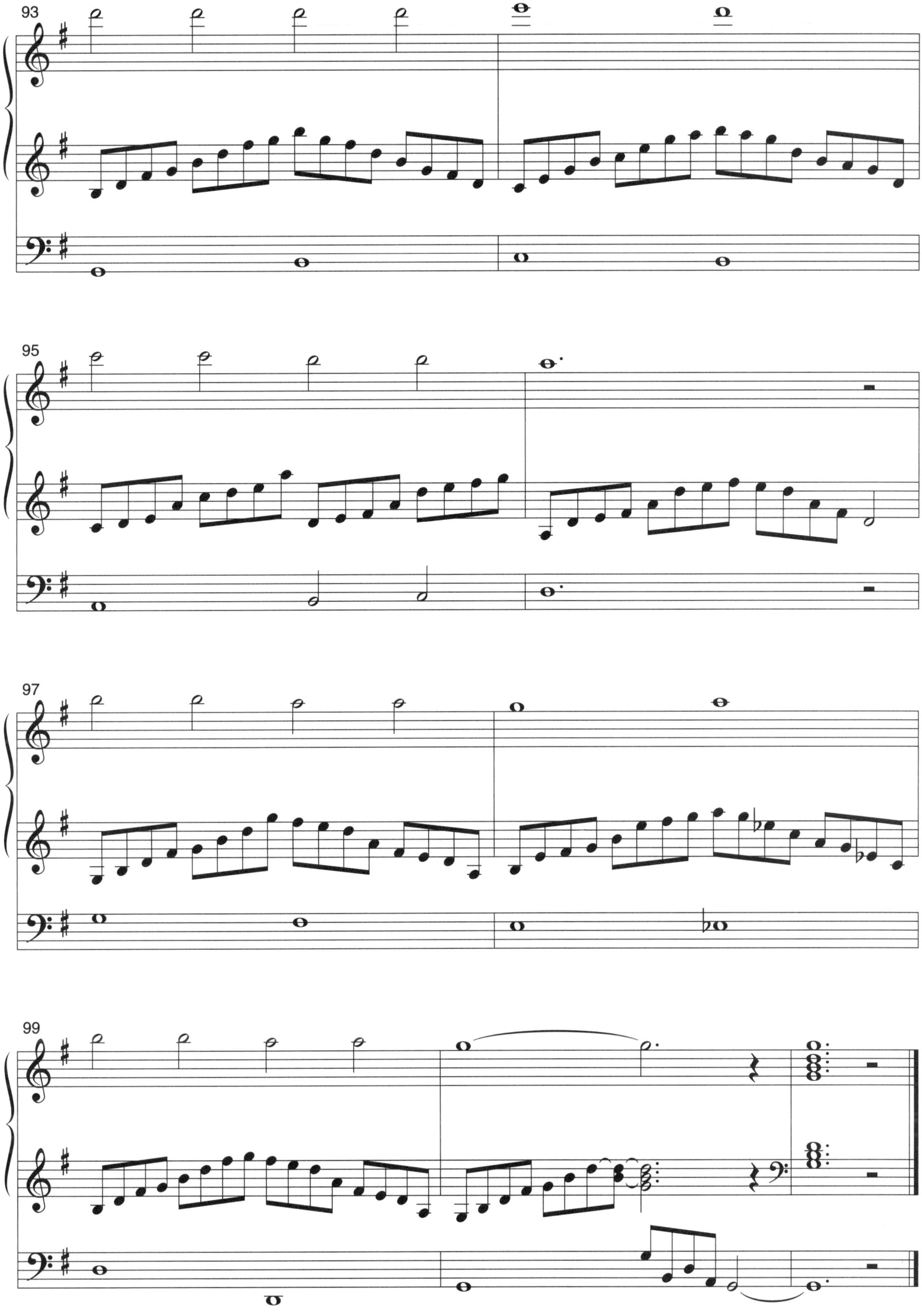
93
95
97
99

to Carolyn,
congratulations on over fifty years of music ministry

HYMN OF MAJESTY AND POWER

General [1]
All strings, flutes and light principals 8' and 4', tremulants, Vox humana, coupled to Choir at 8' and 4' and to Great 16', 8', 4'
Great: Flutes 16', 8', 4'
Pedal: Soft 32', 16', 8', 4' flutes to balance, Sw. to Ped., Ch. to Ped.

General [2]
Principals and Flutes 8', 4', 2', light Mixture
Pedal: Principals and Flutes 16', 8', 4'

General [3]
Add to General [2]: Sw. and Ch. Reeds 16', 8', 4'
Solo: Fanfare Trompette

Swedish Folk Melody
Arranged by MARK THALLANDER

12
Gen. [3]
Boxes
closed
16
f
Solo
ff
19
Add
Mixtures
Gt.
f
22
Gen. [1]
Ch.

26
Gen. [3]
Gt.
f
30
Broadly
Add
Gt. Reeds
ff
33
Triumphantly
rit.
ten.
36
molto rit.
fff
Full Organ
+ Gt. to Ped.
+ 32' Reed

for Carolyn Hamlin in celebration of her golden jubilee

TOCCATA ON "HYMN TO JOY"

LUDWIG VAN BEETHOVEN
Arranged by JOEL MARTINSON

Sw. Principals 8', 4', 2', Mixture, Reeds 8'
Gt. Principals 16', 8', 4', 2', Mixture, Pos. to Gt., Sw. to Gt.
Pos. Principals 8', 4', 2', (low) Mixture, Sw. to Pos.
Ped. Principals 16', 8', 4', Mixture, Reeds 16', 8', 4', Gt. to Ped., Sw. to Ped.

12
16
poco rit.
a tempo
(somewhat detached)
20
legato
23

37
40
43
46
rall.
a tempo

* *The pedal melody may be played in octaves from this point through measure 71, with the exception of mm. 62 to 66 (beat 3).*

60
(no octaves)
63
poco rit.
66
a tempo
(play octaves)
69

Add to all manuals
71
74
77
80
molto rall.
(Right Foot)

in honor of Carolyn Hamlin,
celebrating 50 years as organist at
First Baptist Church - Easley, South Carolina

TOCCATA ON "MENDELSSOHN"

Sw. Full with reeds
Gt. Full through Trumpet 8'
Ch. Full
Ped. Full through reeds 16', 8',
manuals coupled and coupled to Ped.

FELIX MENDELSSOHN
Arranged by CRAIG PHILLIPS

13
17
21
25

28
31
35
39

43
poco rall.
47
breve
mf a tempo
poco non legato
Ch.
reduce Ped.
legato
51
55

59
63
cresc.
Gt.
f
67
Ch.
70

74
Gt.
77
80
Gt.
7
add reeds 16', 8'
84
add
ff

87
poco non legato
add 32' reed
91
95
99

103
107
111
114

117
121
124
127

130
133
fff
fff
136
poco rall.
139
a tempo
rall.

to Carolyn Hamlin, in appreciation of her long and distinguished ministry of music

VARIATIONS ON "ADESTE FIDELES"

JOHN FRANCIS WADE
Arranged by FREDERICK SWANN

These suggested registrations are for a sizeable and colorful organ, but can be adapted to smaller instruments by inventive organists. Please note that the Zimbelstern, indicated for use in measures 1-11 should be used ***only*** if it is under expression and *pp*. It will give the effect of falling snow!

Begin: Swell – Soft celestes 8'
Solo – Flute 4', tremulant
(Prepare Solo [1] – English Horn 8')
Great – Chimes
Zimbelstern

GENERAL [1]
Solo – French Horn 8'
Swell – Principal 8', Flute, Viola
Choir – Flutes 8', 4', 1-1/3'
Pedal – Soft 16' + Swell to Pedal

GENERAL [2]
Solo – Corno di bessetto 8'
Great – Flutes 8, 2'
Choir – Flutes 8', 4', 1-1/3'
Pedal – Soft 16', 8' Flutes

GENERAL [3]
Solo – Strings and Flutes, French Horn
Swell – Strings and Flutes 16', 8', 4'
Vox Humana
Great – Flutes 8', Strings, Diapasons
Swell, Choir, Solo to Great 8', 4'
Choir – Strings and Flutes 8', 4'
Swell to Choir 8'
Pedal – 32', 16', 8' to match, plus
Swell and Choir to Pedal
All tremulants

GENERAL [4]
Solo – *fff* Trumpet or Tuba
Swell, Great, Choir –
Principals, 8', 4', 2'
Sw./Ch. to Great
Swell to Choir
Pedal – 32', 16', 8'
Sw./Gt./Ch. to Pedal
(Prepare Full Swell on a
Swell piston)

GENERAL [5]
Solo – *fff* Trumpet or Tuba
Swell, Great, Choir, Pedal – Full, coupled to Great *and* Pedal 8', 4'

You may also need a General piston to quickly access Harp and Chimes only for measures 55-57.

*It is important to draw the Zimbelstern and have it sound *alone* for a full measure before beginning measure 2 on the Swell.

22
Sw.
(♮)
+ 4', 2'
26
f
Ped.
30
Ch.
34
Gen. [2]
maintain tempo
Solo

37
40
tr
tr
44
5
Gt.
47

50
Ch.
Solo
53
rit.
Harp
56
Very legato (♩ = 80)
Gen. [3]
Ch.
mf
Gt.
f
Chime
rit.
60

64
68
Gen. [4]
poco rit.
Ch.
mf
Gt.
f
72
+ Full Sw.
box closed
cresc.
76
Solo (or fff trumpet)
poco rit.
ff
well articulated
Gen. [5]

80
rit.
Gt.
Breve
83
♩ = 80
a tempo
87
poco rit.
91
Reed
fff

95
tr
Gt.
99
Slowly
poco rit.
102
molto rit.
Full Organ
marcato

to Carolyn Hamilton, whose lifelong service to organ and church music serves as an inspiration to us all

THE PROMISED LAND

The Southern Harmony
Arranged by TREY CLEGG

General [1]
Sw. Festival Trumpet 8'
Gt. Trompette en Chamade 8'
Ch. Tuba 8'
Ped. Principal 16', Sw. to Ped. 8'

General [2]
Sw. Principals 8', 4', 2', Mixture
Gt. Trompette en Chamade 8'
Ch. Principals 8', 4', 2', Mixture
Swell to Choir 8'
Ped. Flute 16'

General [3]
Sw. Flute 8', Nazard 2-2/3', Tierce 1-3/5', Trem.
Ch. Strings 8', 4', Celestes
Ped. Flute 16'

General [4]
All Manuals coupled: Full Organ
Ped. Full with all couplers & 32'

Swell
[1] Principals 8', 4', Flutes 8', 4'
[2] Festival Trumpet 8'
[3] Trompette 8'

Great
[1] Trompette en Chamade 8'

Choir
[1] Tuba 8'
[2] Dulzian 8'

8
Ch.
12
Gt. fff
16
Sw. [2]
ff
Ch. f
Gen. [2]
Ch.
ff
20

24
Gen. [1] Sw.
Gt. fff
28
Gen. [3] Sw.
Ch.
p
31
slowly & expressively
Ch.
35
rit.

39
Ch. [1]
f
Sw. [3]
mf
Ch. [2]
mp
Gen. [1]
Gt. fff
43
Sw.
ff
Ch. f
47
Sw. [1] mf
Ch.
51

55
Sw. [2]
Gt.
59
Ch.
62
Gen. [4]
Gt.
fff
63

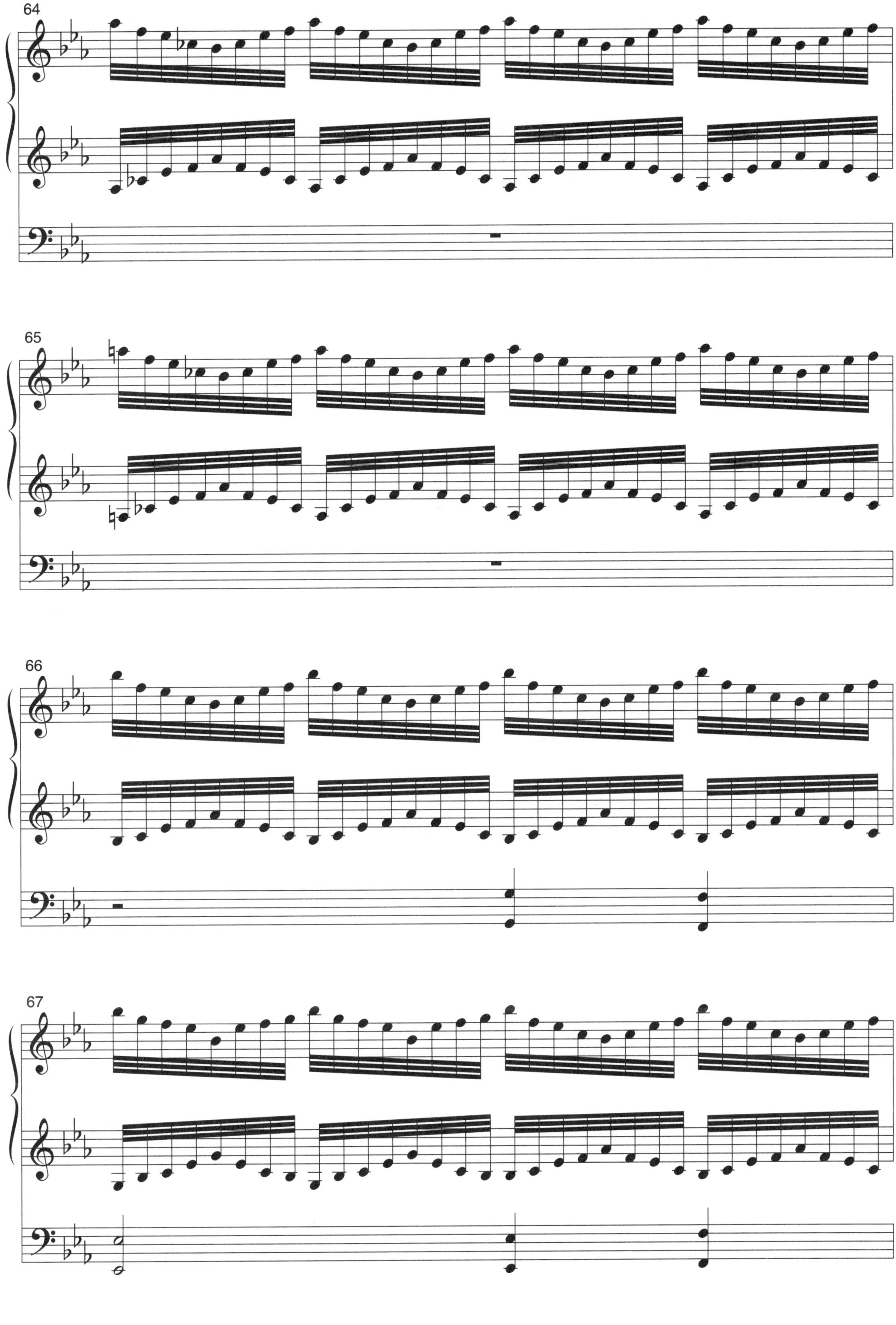
64
65
66
67

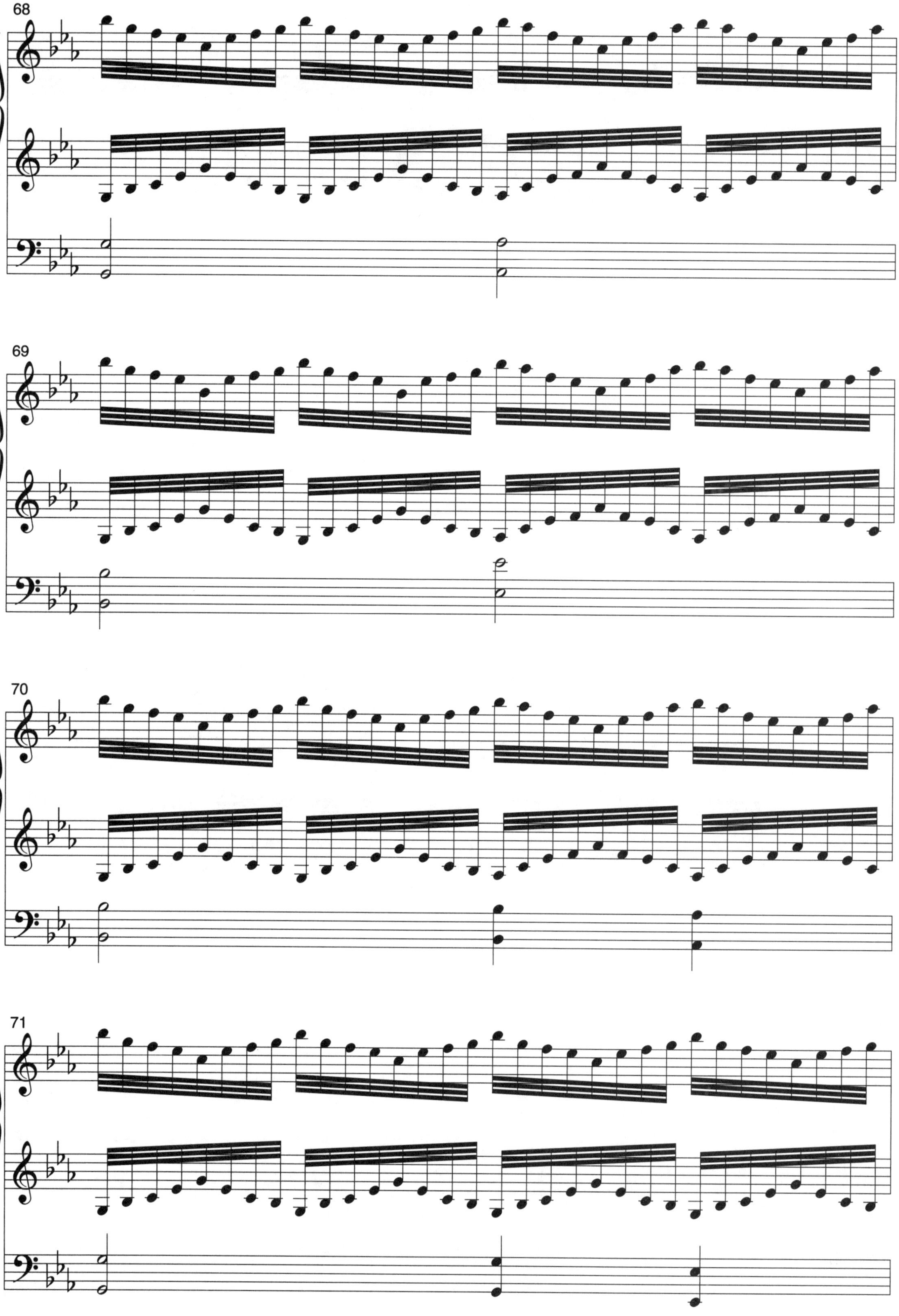
68
69
70
71

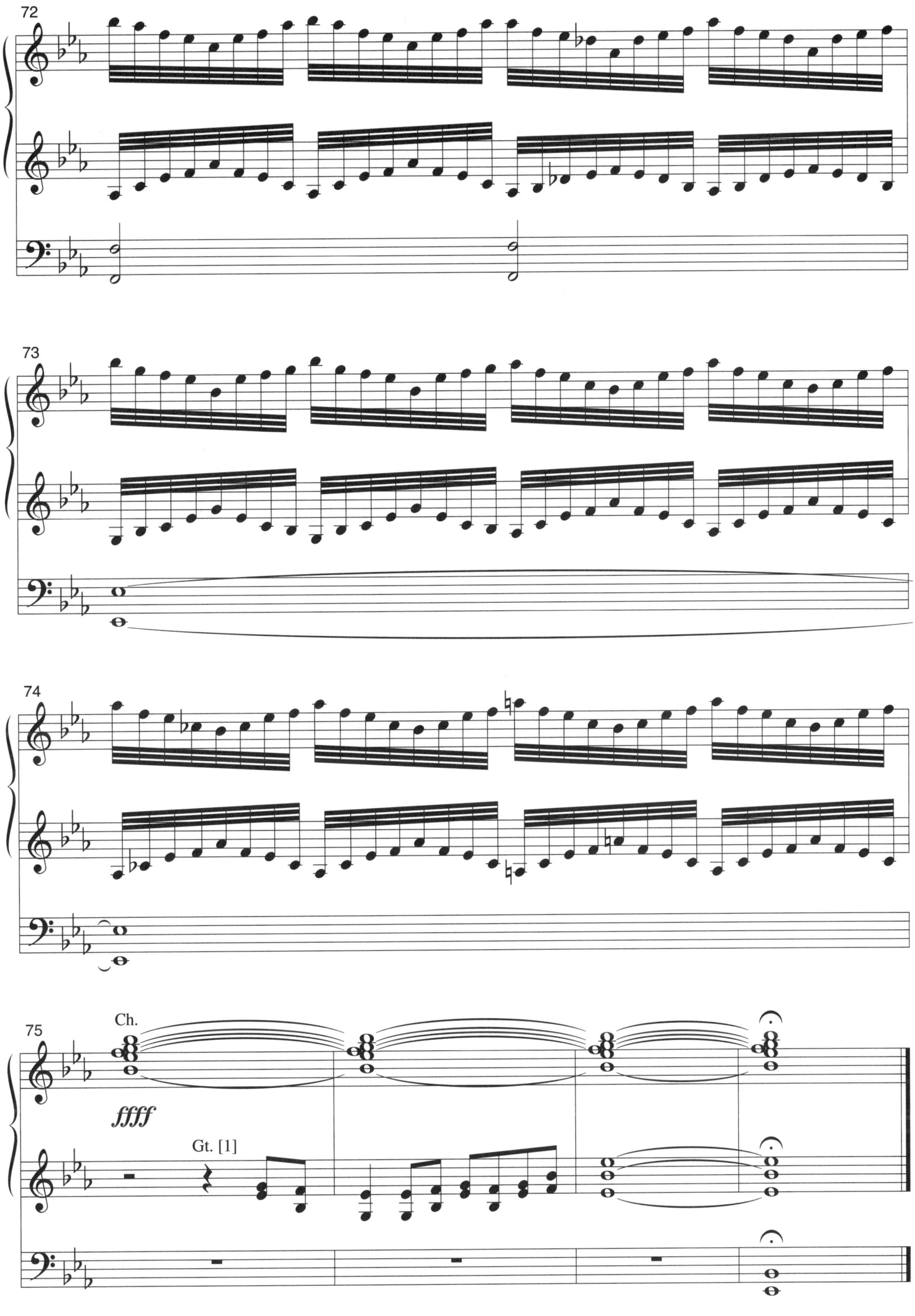
72
73
74
75
Ch.
ffff
Gt. [1]

with honor and respect for my friend, Carolyn Hamlin

AND CAN IT BE

Sw. Strings 8'
Gt. Principals 8', 4', 2' (prepare IV)
Solo: 8'
Ped. Principal 16', 8', 4' (prepare Flutes 16', 8')

THOMAS CAMPBELL
Arranged by ANNA LAURA PAGE

13
17
21
25

29
33
37
41

45
rit. poco a poco
Sw.
mp
Sw.
-4'
Flute 16', 8'
Slower (♩ = ca. 92)
49
mf 8' Solo
(Sw.)
53
57

61
65
Sw.
69
8' Solo
73
Sw.

77
f
81
Tempo I
Gt.
Gt.
Prin. 16', 8', 4'
85
cresc. e rit.
89
Majestically (♩ = ca. 108)
ff

93
97
101
105

109
+IV
113
118
gradual cresc.
123
fff rit.

commissioned in honor of Carolyn Hamlin

THE SOLID ROCK

General [1]
Sw. Foundations 8', 4', 2', Reed 8'
Gt. Foundations 8', 4', 2'
Pos. Solo Trumpet 8'
Ped. Foundations 16', 8'

General [2]
Sw. Flutes 8', 4'
Gt. Flutes 8', 2'
Pos. Krummhorn 8', Flute 4'
Ped. Subbass 16', Gedeckt 8'

General [3]
Sw. Foundations 8', 4', Mixtures, Reed(s) 8, (4')
Gt. Light 16', Foundations 8', 4', Mixtures, Sw. & Pos. to Gt.
Pos. Foundations 8', 4', 2'
Ped. Foundations 16', 8', 4'

WILLIAM B. BRADBURY
Arranged by MICHAEL BURKHARDT

12
16
20
24
Pos.
Sw.

28
Sw.
32
36
Gen. [2]
Gt.
39
Sw.
Gt.
Sw.
simile

43
Sw.
Gt.
47
Sw.
Gt.
51
leggiero
slight rit.
55
a tempo
lingering
Sw.
Pos.

58
62
Gt.
66
70
Pos.

74
78
Gt.
82
Gen. [3]
Sw.
mf
non legato gradual cresc.
86
f
+ Reed 16',
Sw. to Ped.

90
Gt.
93
96
99

102
rit.
105
a tempo
108
rit.
a tempo
rit.
+ 32'

to Carolyn Hamlin, with congratulations on your music and ministry

NOW THANK WE ALL OUR GOD

Sw. Strings 16', 8', 4'
Gt. Flutes 8', 4', Sw. & Ch. to Gt. 8'
Ch. Strings 8', 4', Sw. to Ch. 16', 8', 4'
Ped. Bourdon 16', Subbass 16', Sw. to Ped.

JOHANN CRÜGER
Arranged by DIANE BISH

12
16
Gt.
- Sw. to Ch. 16' + Ch. Flute 8'
3 3 3 3
- Bourdon 32'
19
simile
22

25
28
+ Small Foundation 8'
31
34
rit.
a tempo

37
+ Foundation 8', 4'
+ Mixture
+ Sw. Reeds
16', 8', 4'
gradual cresc.
Gt.
broaden
39
a tempo
ff
41
simile
43

45
47
49
51

53
55
rit.
56
a tempo
gradual cresc.
58
broaden
fff